PLAY BALL!

QUOTES ON AMERICA'S FAVORITE PASTIME

PLAY BALL!

QUOTES ON AMERICA'S
FAVORITE PASTIME

ARIEL BOOKS

ANDREWS AND MCMEEL
KANSAS CITY

ISBN: 0-8362-0721-1
Library of Congress Catalog Card Number: 95-76437

First Printing, September 1995
Second Printing, March 1996

INTRODUCTION

It is an American institution and more lasting than some marriages, war, Supreme Court decisions, and even major depressions.

—ART RUST, INDIANS THIRD BASEMAN

Americans have loved and followed baseball since the mid-nineteenth century, and can't imagine life without it. It is our national pastime, but, more than that, it is part of our culture. The game's unhurried pace offers a refreshing contrast to our otherwise fast-paced existence. Baseball brings a constancy to our lives. There will always be die-hard fans, baseball cards, irate managers arguing with frustrated umpires, and, of course, words of wit and wisdom written about the game: more words probably than any other sport. Players, managers, owners, fans, critics—they all have something to say about the pleasures of a well-executed steal, a perfect suicide squeeze, or a home run shot to center field. And, of course, they always have plenty to say about the disappointments of a batting slump, a favorite player who's traded to another team, or a pitcher who loses the game in the ninth inning.

Baseball has been blessed by the wit, sometimes unintentional, of Yogi Berra ("I really didn't say everything I said"), Dizzy Dean, Bill Veeck, and Tommy Lasorda. The game has been given eloquence by Lou Gehrig, Willie Mays, and Bart Giamatti, and a homespun philosophy by Satchel Paige, Leo Durocher, and Connie Mack who said, "You can't win them all." What sport but baseball could give us a five-word phrase that sums up not only an important lesson of the game but also of life?

This book collects the best-known, funniest, and wisest malapropisms, aphorisms, jibes, musings, and epithets that are as integral to the game as rain delays, night games, and spring training. As Ronald Reagan said about playing baseball, "This is really more fun than being president."

Baseball was, is and always will be to me the best game in the world.

BABE RUTH
Yankees outfielder

There are three things the average man thinks he can do better than anybody else: build a fire, run a hotel, and manage a baseball team.

ROCKY BRIDGES
major league utility man

A hot dog at the ballpark is better than steak at the Ritz.

HUMPHREY BOGART

actor

Baseball to me is still the national pastime because it is a summer game. I feel that almost all Americans are summer people, that summer is what they think of when they think of their childhood. I think it stirs up an incredible emotion within people.

STEVE BUSBY
Royals pitcher

The first big-league game I ever saw was at the Polo Grounds. My father took me. I remember it so well—the green grass and the green stands. It was like seeing Oz.

JOHN CURTIS
Giants pitcher

You can't hit what you can't see.

WALTER JOHNSON
Senators pitcher
(describing his pitching strategy)

It's great to be young and a Yankee.

WAITE HOYT
Yankees pitcher

Losing streaks are funny. If you lose at the beginning, you got off to a bad start. If you lose in the middle of the season, you're in a slump. If you lose at the end, you're choking.

GENE MAUCH
Phillies manager

The best thing about being a Yankee is getting to watch Reggie Jackson play every day. The worst thing about being a Yankee? Getting to watch Reggie Jackson play every day.

GRAIG NETTLES
Yankees third baseman

One reason I never called balks is that I never understood the rule.

RON LUCIANO
American League umpire

If you're not having fun in baseball, you miss the point of everything.

CHRIS CHAMBLISS
Braves first baseman

You don't face Ryan without your rest. He's the only guy I go against that makes me go to bed before midnight.

REGGIE JACKSON
Yankees outfielder
(on Nolan Ryan)

My high salary for one season was forty-six thousand dollars and a Cadillac. If I were to get paid a million, I'd feel that I should sweep out the stadium every night after I finished playing the game.

DUKE SNIDER
Dodgers outfielder

Throwing people out of a game is like learning to ride a bicycle—once you get the hang of it, it can be a lot of fun.

RON LUCIANO
American League umpire

When I was a small boy in Kansas, a friend of mine and I went fishing . . . I told him I wanted to be a real major league baseball player, a genuine professional like Honus Wagner. My friend said that he'd like to be President of the United States. Neither of us got our wish.

DWIGHT D. EISENHOWER
*thirty-fourth president
of the United States*

The whole history of baseball has the quality of mythology.

BERNARD MALAMUD
author

It's a strange
business, all jeers
and no cheers.

TOM GORMAN
National League umpire

There'll be two buses leaving the hotel for the park tomorrow. The two o'clock bus will be for those of you who need a little extra work. The empty bus will leave at five o'clock.

DAVE BRISTOL
Brewers manager

The hitter asks the owner to give him a big raise so he can go somewhere he's never been, and the owner says, "You mean third base."

HENNY YOUNGMAN
comedian

Pitching is the art of instilling fear.

SANDY KOUFAX
Dodgers pitcher

It's worth remembering, that under Steinbrenner we tend to operate on the theory that no one is unsignable.

A YANKEE SCOUT
(overheard trying to lure John Elway away from football)

Baseball has no penalties at all. A home run is a home run. You cheer. In football, on a score, you look for flags. If there's one, who's it on? When can we cheer? Football acts can be repealed. Baseball acts stand forever.

THOMAS BOSWELL
author

Baseball is a public trust. Players turn over, owners turn over and certain commissioners turn over. But baseball goes on.

PETER UEBERROTH
baseball commissioner

Say it ain't so, Joe.

ANONYMOUS
*(a little boy who pleaded with Joe Jackson
after the airing of the 1920 "Black Sox"
scandal)*

WILL THE LAST PERSON TO LEAVE THE STADIUM PLEASE TURN OUT THE LIGHTS

---

sign held by a fan at Wrigley Field in Chicago at the end of the first complete night game

Well, baseball was my whole life. Nothing's ever been as fun as baseball.

MICKEY MANTLE
Yankees outfielder

I'm working on a new pitch. It's called a strike.

JIM KERN
Indians relief pitcher

You always get a special kick on opening day, no matter how many you go through. You look forward to it like a birthday party when you're a kid. You think something wonderful is going to happen.

JOE DIMAGGIO
Yankees outfielder

I never slept when I lost. I'd see the sun come up without ever having closed my eyes. I'd see those base hits over and over and they'd drive me crazy.

ROBIN ROBERTS
Phillies pitcher

Spring is the time of year when the ground thaws, trees bud, the income tax falls due—and everybody wins the pennant.

JIM MURRAY
sportswriter

I don't want them to forget Ruth. I just want them to remember me!

HANK AARON
Braves outfielder

The sport to which I owe so much has undergone profound changes . . . but it's still baseball. Kids still imitate their heroes on playgrounds. Fans still ruin expensive suits going after foul balls that cost five dollars. Hitting streaks still make the network news. And the hot dogs still taste better at the ballpark than at home.

DUKE SNIDER
Dodgers outfielder

You can shake a dozen glove men out of a tree, but the bat separates the men from the boys.

DALE LONG
Senators first baseman

Every day in every way, baseball gets fancier. A few more years and they'll be playing on oriental rugs.

RUSSELL BAKER
columnist

To say 'Babe Ruth' is to say 'Baseball.'

WILL HARRIDGE
American League president

Baseball is all clean lines and clear decisions . . . wouldn't life be far easier if it consisted of a series of definitive calls; safe or out, fair or foul, strike or ball. Oh, for a life like that, where every day produces a clear winner and an equally clear loser, and back to it the next day with the slate wiped clean and the teams starting out equal.

ERIC ROLFE GREENBERG
author

I believe managing is like holding a dove in your hand. If you hold it too tightly, you kill it, but if you hold it too loosely, you lose it.

TOMMY LASORDA
Dodgers manager

A ballplayer has two reputations, one with the other players and one with the fans. The first is based on ability. The second the newspapers give him.

JOHNNY EVERS
Cubs infielder

The main idea is to win.

JOHN J. McGRAW
Giants manager

I try not to break the rules but merely to test their elasticity.

BILL VEECK
baseball executive

The most exciting hit in baseball is the triple. . . . You usually have two or three men handling the ball; and, if everything fits together, the runner is flagged down on a close play. On doubles and triples, several men must contribute. On a home run, one man does it all.

HARRY WALKER
Astros manager

Umpire's heaven is a place where he works third base every game. Home is where the heartache is.

RON LUCIANO
American League umpire

Your bat is your life. It's your weapon. You don't want to go into battle with anything that feels less than perfect.

LOU BROCK
Cardinals outfielder

Every day is a new opportunity. You can build on yesterday's success or put its failures behind and start over again. That's the way life is, with a new game every day, and that's the way baseball is.

BOB FELLER
Indians pitcher

You see, you spend a good piece of your life gripping a baseball, and in the end it turns out that it was the other way around all the time.

JIM BOUTON
major league pitcher

I love baseball. It's given me everything I have. Look, there are only about six hundred major leaguers in the country. You have to feel special.

THURMAN MUNSON
Yankees catcher

Under the circumstances, I wouldn't have the job [of baseball commissioner today]. It's impossible to do it. Every time the commissioner makes a decision, he's in court. Every player has an agent; every club owner has a lawyer. The game has left the field and gone to court.

A. B. (HAPPY) CHANDLER
baseball commissioner

I've never taken batting practice against him and I never will. I have a family to think of.

BOB WATSON
Astros first baseman
(on teammate J. R. Richard)

Every season has its peaks and valleys. What you have to try to do is eliminate the Grand Canyon.

ANDY VAN SLYKE
Pirates outfielder

The only mistake I made in my whole baseball career was hitting .361 that one year (1961), because ever since then people have expected me to keep on doing it.

NORM CASH
Tigers first baseman

I was pitching on all adrenaline . . . and challenging them. I was throwing the ball right down the heart of the plate.

ROGER CLEMENS
Red Sox pitcher
(on striking out 20 batters
in a nine-inning game)

When you're going good it doesn't get any better than being in New York. But when you're going bad, it doesn't get any worse.

DAVEY JOHNSON
Mets manager

When you get on first, know you are going to second. Know you can beat the pitcher and the catcher and the two of them combined. You have to have an inner conceit to be a successful base stealer. You have to know you are better than either the pitcher or the catcher.

PETE REISER
Dodgers coach

Catching a fly ball is a pleasure.
But knowing what to do with it after
you catch it is a business.

TOMMY HENRICH
Yankees outfielder

Whoever wants to know the heart and mind of America had better learn baseball, the rules and realities of the game—and do it by watching first some high school or small-town teams.

JACQUES BARZUN
author

Carlton does not pitch to the hitter, he pitches through him. The batter hardly exists for Steve. He's playing an elevated game of catch.

TIM McCARVER
Cardinals catcher

One of the chief duties of the fan is to engage in arguments with the man behind him. This department has been allowed to run down fearfully.

ROBERT BENCHLEY
author

I was the worst hitter ever. I never even broke a bat until last year. That was backing out of the garage.

LEFTY GOMEZ
Yankees pitcher

Boys, baseball is a game where you gotta have fun. You do that by winning.

DAVE BRISTOL
Reds manager

If you aim to steal 30 or 40 bases a year, you do it by surprising the other side. But if your goal is 50 to 100 bases, the element of surprise doesn't matter. You go even though they know you're going to go. Then each steal becomes a contest, matching your skills against theirs.

LOU BROCK
Cardinals outfielder

You gotta be a man to play baseball for a living but you gotta have a lot of little boy in you, too.

ROY CAMPANELLA
Dodgers catcher

Dickey is teaching me all his experiences.

YOGI BERRA
*Yankees catcher
(on learning about catching
from Bill Dickey)*

I am the best in baseball. . . . I create an excitement in a ballpark when I walk on the field.

REGGIE JACKSON
Yankees outfielder

I wanted to be a big league base-ball player so I could see my picture on a bubble gum card.

AL FERRARA
Dodgers outfielder

When asked by a Canadian customs agent if he had anything to declare, Steve Foster of the Reds answered: "Sure. I'm proud to be an American."

STEVE FOSTER
Reds pitcher

Baseball is a lot like life. The line drives are caught, the squibbers go for base hits. It's an unfair game.

ROD KANEHL
Mets infielder

There were times last year when people looked at the scoreboard and thought my batting average was the temperature.

BUCK MARTINEZ
Blue Jays catcher
(on his .162 performance)

When I began playing the game, baseball was as gentlemanly as a kick in the crotch.

TY COBB
Tigers outfielder

Maybe I'm not a great man, but I damn well want to break the record.

ROGER MARIS
Yankees outfielder

If I had my career to play over, one thing I'd do differently is swing more. Those 1,200 walks I got—nobody remembers them.

PEE WEE REESE
Dodgers shortstop

It's designed to break your heart. The game begins in the spring, when everything else begins again, and it blossoms in the summer, filling the afternoons and evenings, and then as soon as the chill rains come, it stops, and leaves you to face the fall alone.

A. BARTLETT GIAMATTI
baseball commissioner

Everything looks nicer when you win. The girls are prettier. The cigars taste better. The trees are greener.

BILLY MARTIN
Yankees manager

One of the beautiful things about
baseball is that every once in a while
you come into a situation where you
want to, and where you have to,
reach down and prove something.

NOLAN RYAN
Astros pitcher

Baseball players are smarter than football players. How often do you see a baseball team penalized for too many men on the field?

JIM BOUTON
Yankees pitcher

I don't think we had the pressures then that ballplayers have now, because there was no television.

RALPH KINER
television announcer

Baseball is beautiful . . . the supreme performing art. It combines in perfect harmony the magnificent features of ballet, drama, art, and ingenuity.

BOWIE KUHN
baseball commissioner

Baseball gives you every chance to be great. Then it puts the pressure on you to prove that you haven't got what it takes. It never takes away the chance, and it never eases up on the pressure.

JOE GARAGIOLA
Cardinals catcher

No matter how many errors you make, no matter how many times you strike out, keep hustling. That way you'll at least look like a ballplayer.

TONY KUBEK, SR.
(to his son, Yankee rookie Tony Kubek, Jr.)

There are only five things you can do in baseball—run, throw, catch, hit and hit with power.

LEO DUROCHER
baseball executive

A baseball club is part of the chemistry of the city. A game isn't just an athletic contest. It's a picnic, a kind of town meeting.

MICHAEL BURKE
Yankees president

When I think of a stadium, it's like a temple. It's religious.

JIM LEFEBVRE
Giants coach

The difference between relief pitching when I did it and today is simple: there's too much of it. It's one of those cases where more is not necessarily better.

BOB FELLER
Indians pitcher

From the start catching appealed to me as a chance to be in the thick of the game continuously. I never had to be lonely behind the plate where I could talk to the hitters. I also learned that by engaging them in conversation I could sometimes distract them.

ROY CAMPANELLA
Dodgers catcher

The only people I ever felt intimidated by in my whole life were Bob Gibson and my daddy.

DUSTY BAKER
Giants manager and former Dodgers star

That's what it means to be an umpire. You have to be honest even when it hurts.

DOUG HARVEY
National League umpire
(on errors)

If I were playing third base and my mother were rounding third with the run that was going to beat us, I'd trip her. Oh, I'd pick her up and brush her off and say, "Sorry, Mom," but nobody beats me.

LEO DUROCHER
baseball executive

Baseball? It's just a game—as simple as a ball and a bat. Yet, as complex as the American spirit it symbolizes. It's a sport, business— and sometimes even religion.

ERNIE HARWALL
broadcaster

The playoffs are the wedge between the season and the World Series. If you lose, it means you won't be going to the greatest sports event in this country. It's the quagmire before the promised land. It's the Red Sea that has to be crossed. If you don't cross into the World Series, you're a loser. You're forgotten by Thanksgiving.

TIM MCCARVER
Cardinals catcher

On any given day . . . come out to the ballpark and you'll see something different.

FRED BORSCH
sportswriter

I was not successful as a ball-player, as it was a game of skill.

CASEY STENGEL
baseball executive

My ultimate dream is to have my own bank, maybe in Paris. I'd call it Banks' Bank on the Left Bank.

ERNIE BANKS
Cubs shortstop

There is magic in the moment, for when I open my eyes and see my sons in the place where my father once sat, I feel an invisible bond between our three generations, an anchor of loyalty linking my sons to the grandfather whose face they never saw but whose person they have already come to know through this most timeless of all sports, baseball.

DORIS KEARNS GOODWIN
author

I want to be remembered as a ballplayer who gave all he had to give.

ROBERTO CLEMENTE
Pirates outfielder

The bases were drunk and I painted the black with my best yakker. But blue squeezed me, and I went full. I came back with my heater, but the stick flares one the other way and chalk flies for two bases. Three earnies! Next thing I know, skipper hooks me and I'm sipping suds with the clubby.

ED LYNCH
Mets pitcher

Age is a question of mind over matter. If you don't mind, age don't matter.

SATCHEL PAIGE
Negro league pitcher

I don't know anything about ballet, but I wish people would watch baseball the way ballet fans watch the dance—not to see who wins but to see how well each player performs his part.

MIKE MARSHALL
Dodgers pitcher

The two most important things in life are good friends and a strong bullpen.

BOB LEMON
Yankees manager

Not making the baseball team at West Point was one of the greatest disappointments of my life, maybe the greatest.

DWIGHT D. EISENHOWER
*thirty-fourth president
of the United States*

The new definition of a heathen is a man who has never played baseball.

ELBERT HUBBARD
author

I'm no different from anybody else with two arms, two legs, and forty-two hundred hits.

PETE ROSE
Reds infielder

Well, God is certainly getting an earful tonight.

JIM MURRAY
sportswriter
(on Casey Stengel's death)

A critic once characterized baseball as six minutes of action crammed into two-and-one-half hours.

RAY FITZGERALD
sportswriter

I don't know what it is. The big crowds. The hundreds of reporters, photographers and television men. The flags decorating the stadium. . . . Whatever it is, you suddenly feel the excitement of it all and nothing that happened before is important.

BOB GIBSON
Cardinals pitcher

I played baseball because I could make more money doing that than I could doing anything else.

BILL TERRY

Giants first baseman

My place is at Mom's side. She is worth more to me than any ball game or any World Series that was ever invented.

LOU GEHRIG
*Yankees first baseman
(on staying at his sick mother's bedside
when Yankee manager Miller Huggins
asked him to play in the 1927 series)*

The World Series is American sport's annual ticket to a romantic yesterday, when we were all young and surely going to be in the big leagues someday.

RAY FITZGERALD
sportswriter

No baseball fan has to explain his mania to any other baseball fan. They are a fraternity. It is less easy, often it is hopeless, to try to explain it to anyone else. You grow technical, and you do not make sense. You grow sentimental, and you are deemed soft in the head. How, the benighted outsider asks you with no little condescension, can you grow sentimental about a cold-blooded professional sport?

JOHN K. HUTCHENS
author

No game in the world is as tidy and dramatically neat as baseball, with cause and effect, crime and punishment, motive and result, so cleanly defined.

PAUL GALLICO
author

Ballplayers who are first into the dining room are usually last in the averages.

JIMMY CANNON
sportswriter

The secret of managing is to keep the guys who hate you away from the guys who are undecided.

CASEY STENGEL
Mets manager

It helps a pitcher to be exposed to the enemy camp.

AL DOWNING
major league pitcher
(on why he rooms with batters
while traveling)

Why pitch nine innings when you can get just as famous pitching two?

SPARKY LYLE
Yankees relief pitcher

All literary men are Red Sox fans—to be a Yankee fan in a literate society is to endanger your life.

JOHN CHEEVER
author

These moments are the soul of baseball: the ball perfectly hit, perfectly caught, or perfectly thrown. . . . We can unwrap the moments later, when it's quiet, and enjoy them all over again.

ALISON GORDON
author

Swing at the strikes.

YOGI BERRA
Yankees catcher

Kids today are looking for idols, but sometimes they look too far . . . They don't have to look any farther than their home because those are the people that love you. They are the real heroes.

BOBBY BONILLA
Pirates third baseman

Fans don't boo nobodies.

REGGIE JACKSON
Yankees outfielder

What's important is that baseball, after twenty-eight years of artificial turf and expansion and the designated hitter and drugs and free agency and thousand-dollar bubble gum cards, is still a gift given by fathers to sons.

MICHAEL CHABON
author

Baseball is ninety percent mental. The other half is physical.

YOGI BERRA
Yankees catcher

Back then, if you had a sore arm, the only people concerned were you and your wife. Now, it's you, your wife, your agent, your investment counselor, your stockbroker, and your publisher.

JIM BOUTON
Yankees pitcher

Baseball is green and safe. It has neither the street intimidation of basketball nor the controlled Armageddon of football. . . . Baseball is a green dream that happens on summer nights in safe places in unsafe cities.

LUKE SALISBURY
author

You must have an alibi to show why you lost. If you haven't one, you must fake one. Your self-confidence must be maintained.

CHRISTY MATHEWSON
Giants pitcher

Trying to throw a fastball by Hank Aaron is like trying to sneak the sun past a rooster.

CURT SIMMONS
Phillies pitcher

Everybody judges players different. I judge a player by what he does for his ball club and not by what he does for himself. I think the name of the game is self-sacrifice.

BILLY MARTIN
Twins manager

I don't like to sound egotistical, but every time I stepped to the plate with a bat in my hands, I couldn't help but feel sorry for the pitcher.

ROGERS HORNSBY
Cardinals infielder

Two events are supremely beautiful: the strikeout and the home run. Each is a difficult and unlikely thing flawlessly achieved before your eyes.

WILLIAM SAROYAN
author

When the ball is over the middle of the plate, the batter is hitting it with the sweet part of the bat. When it's inside, he's hitting it with the part of the bat from the handle to the trademark; when it's outside, he's hitting it with the end of the bat. You've got to keep the ball away from the sweet part of the bat. To do that the pitcher has to move the hitter off the plate.

DON DRYSDALE
Dodgers pitcher

It ain't over 'til it's over.

YOGI BERRA
Mets manager
(on the 1973 pennant race)

Baseball is the only thing besides the paper clip that hasn't changed.

BILL VEECK
baseball executive

Baseball is the only field of endeavor where a man can succeed three times out of ten and be considered a good performer.

TED WILLIAMS
Red Sox outfielder

If Satch and I were pitching on the same team, we'd cinch the pennant by July 4 and go fishing until World Series time.

DIZZY DEAN
Cardinals pitcher
(on Satchel Paige)

Winning makes you happy all day.

JIMMY WYNN
Dodgers outfielder

There never is any set way to pitch to a great hitter. If there were, he'd be hitting .220.

DON DRYSDALE
Dodgers pitcher

Sometimes I would do just the opposite of what George wanted me to do, because I won't let anyone tell me how to manage. If I'm going down the tube, I'm going to do it my way.

BILLY MARTIN
Yankees manager

Whether you want to or not, you do serve as a role model. People will always put more faith in baseball players than anyone else.

BROOKS ROBINSON
Orioles third baseman

I never look back. I love baseball and you have to be patient and take the good with the bad. After all, it's only a game.

TOM YAWKEY
baseball executive

Some people give their bodies to science; I give mine to baseball.

RON HUNT
major league infielder
(on being hit by a record 243 pitches during his career)

The only real way to know you've been fired is when you arrive at the ballpark and find your name has been scratched from the parking list.

BILLY MARTIN
Yankees manager

The ball once struck off,
Away flies the boy
To the next destined post,
And then home with joy.

ANONYMOUS

One of my goals in life was to be surrounded by unpretentious, rich young men. Then I bought the Braves and I was surrounded by twenty-five of them.

TED TURNER
Braves owner

Baseball is dull only to dull minds.

RED SMITH
sportswriter

Other sports play once a week . . . but this sport is with us every day.

PETER UEBERROTH
baseball commissioner

There should be a new way to record standings in this league: one column for wins, one for losses and one for gifts.

GENE MAUCH
Phillies manager

If he were playing in New York, there'd be a 5'8" statue of him in Times Square.

ANDY MACPHAIL
Twins manager
(on Kirby Puckett)

The best thing
about baseball is
that you can do
something about
yesterday tomorrow.

MANNY TRILLO
Phillies infielder

153

Baseball is like church. Many attend. Few understand.

LEO DUROCHER

baseball executive

I couldn't see well enough to play when I was a boy, so they gave me a special job—they made me the umpire.

HARRY S. TRUMAN
thirty-third president of the United States

I'm waiting for the day we see the "wave" at the Metropolitan Opera.

AL MICHAELS
broadcaster

They say you have to be good to be lucky, but I think you have to be lucky to be good.

RICO CARTY
Braves outfielder

Two-thirds of the earth is covered by water, the other one-third is covered by Garry Maddox.

RALPH KINER
Mets announcer

Baseball is the very symbol, the outward and visible expression of the drive and push and rush and struggle of the raging, tearing, booming nineteenth century.

MARK TWAIN
author

I would have jumped off a tall building. But the way I'm batting, I wouldn't have hit the ground.

PHIL GARNER
Dodgers third baseman
(describing a slump)

The great thing about baseball is that there's a crisis every day.

GABE PAUL
Yankees president

The ball is smaller, the planets are in line, the hole in the ozone layer is bigger, and so is Juan Gonzalez.

TERRY MULHOLLAND
Phillies pitcher
(on why more home runs are
being hit these days)

I think I have already signed some scrap of paper for every man, woman, and child in the United States. What do they do with all those scraps of paper with my signature on it?

VIDA BLUE
Giants pitcher

Man may penetrate the outer reaches of the universe, he may solve the very secret of eternity itself, but for me, the ultimate human experience is to witness the flawless execution of a hit-and-run.

BRANCH RICKEY
baseball executive

Baseball and football are very different games. In a way, both of them are easy. Football is easy if you're crazy as hell. Baseball is easy if you've got patience. They'd both be easier for me if I were a little more crazy—and a little more patient.

BO JACKSON
Royals outfielder, Raiders running back

It's hard to win a pennant, but it's harder losing one.

CHUCK TANNER
Pirates manager

Do they leave it there during games?

BILL LEE
Red Sox pitcher
(upon first seeing Fenway's
37-foot-high left-field wall)

If I played there, they'd name a candy bar after me.

REGGIE JACKSON
A's outfielder
(on New York)

Managing is getting paid for home runs someone else hits.

CASEY STENGEL
Yankees manager

When you win, you eat better, sleep better, and your beer tastes better. And your wife looks like Gina Lollobrigida.

JOHNNY PESKY
Red Sox manager

The only way I'm going to win a Gold Glove is with a can of spray paint.

REGGIE JACKSON
Yankees outfielder
(on his fielding skills)

When asked why he got married in a ballpark, Mookie Wilson said, "My wife wanted a big diamond."

MOOKIE WILSON
Mets outfielder

Wait until Tommy meets the Lord and finds out that He's wearing pinstripes.

GAYLORD PERRY
Giants pitcher
(on Tommy Lasorda's belief that
God wears Dodger blue)

I never threw an illegal pitch. The trouble is, once in a while I toss one that ain't never been seen by this generation.

SATCHEL PAIGE
Negro league pitcher

The last time Willie Mays dropped a pop fly he had a rattle in one hand and a bonnet on his head.

JIM MURRAY
sportswriter

The highlight of your season is
taking the team picture, knowing
that the trading deadline has passed
and you're part of the club.

JOE GARAGIOLA
Cardinals catcher

Baseball is almost the only orderly thing in a very unorderly world. If you get three strikes, even the best lawyer in the world can't get you off.

BILL VEECK
White Sox owner

Look, I like hitting fourth and I like the good batting average. But what I do every day behind the plate is a lot more important because it touches so many more people and so many more aspects of the game.

THURMAN MUNSON
Yankees catcher

Houston used to be an R&R town—rest and relaxation. It's still an R&R town—Ryan and Richard—but that's not exactly rest and relaxation.

LARRY BOWA
Phillies shortstop
(on Nolan Ryan and J. R. Richard)

Trying to hit him is like trying to eat Jell-O with chopsticks.

BOBBY MURCER
Yankees outfielder
(on knuckleballer Phil Niekro)

Experience is a
hard teacher because
she gives the test
first, the lesson
afterward.

VERNON LAW
Pirates pitcher

If my uniform doesn't get dirty, I haven't done anything in the baseball game.

RICKEY HENDERSON
Athletics outfielder

If I'm going to be struck out, that's the way to go. It may sound strange, but I actually enjoyed that. It was like a surgeon's knife—quick and painless.

REGGIE SMITH
Dodgers outfielder
(on being struck out by Nolan Ryan)

Statistics are to baseball what a flaky crust is to Mom's apple pie.

HARRY REASONER
journalist

Putting lights in Wrigley Field is like putting aluminum siding on the Sistine Chapel.

ROGER SIMON
columnist

Bob Gibson is the luckiest pitcher I ever saw. He always pitches when the other team doesn't score any runs.

TIM MCCARVER
Cardinals catcher
(on teammate Gibson)

It's the only occupation where a man has to be perfect the first day on the job and then improve over the years.

ED RUNGE
American League umpire

In order to be an outstanding base-stealer, you have to eliminate the fear of failure. It's like being a safecracker. You can't be down there on your knees turning around every second to see if somebody's looking.

MAURY WILLS
Mariners manager

Trying to hit him was like trying to drink coffee with a fork.

WILLIE STARGELL
Pirates first baseman
(on Sandy Koufax)

September is
pantyhose month.
No nonsense.

DAVE PARKER
Pirates outfielder

190

Most coaches remain anonymous until they screw up. If a third base coach goes the entire season without being interviewed after a game, it means he had a perfect season.

JAY JOHNSTONE
author

Sometimes I look on Roy as my nephew, but sometimes only as my sister's son.

GENE MAUCH
major league manager
(on his nephew Roy Smalley's
inconsistency as a major league
shortstop)

Baseball is just the great American pastime. . . . I get caught up in what I'd do if I were managing.

GEORGE BUSH
forty-first president
of the United States

I

know, but I had a better year
than Hoover.

BABE RUTH

Yankees outfielder
(spoken in response to a reporter's
statement that Babe Ruth's 1930 salary
of $80,000 was higher than the
president's salary of $75,000)

A good groundskeeper can help you win a dozen games a year. He is the tenth man in the lineup.

LOU BOUDREAU
Indians manager

Every great batter works on the theory that the pitcher is more afraid of him than he is of the pitcher.

TY COBB
Tigers outfielder

Baseball, like cricket, is an elegant and leisurely summer game during which tension builds up slowly.

U.S. TRAVEL BROCHURE

... like those special afternoons in summer when you go to Yankee Stadium at two o'clock in the afternoon for an eight o'clock game. It's so big, so empty, and so silent that you can almost hear the sounds that aren't there.

RAY MILLER
Pirates coach

An umpire is like a woman. He makes quick decisions, never reverses them, and doesn't think you're safe when you're out.

LARRY GOETZ
National League umpire

Every player, in his secret heart, wants to manage someday. Every fan, in the privacy of his mind, already does.

LEONARD KOPPETT
author

Is baseball a business? If it isn't, General Motors is a sport.

JIM MURRAY
sportswriter

Open the window,
Aunt Minnie—here
it comes.

ROSEY ROSEWELL
Pirates sportscaster
(on home runs)

I find baseball fascinating. . . . Next to a triple play, baseball's double play is the most exciting and graceful thing in sports.

A L I S T A I R   C O O K E
journalist

You know what Rogers Hornsby told me forty-five years ago? It was the best batting advice I ever got. "Get a good ball to hit."

TED WILLIAMS
Red Sox outfielder

I don't want to play golf. When I hit a ball, I want someone else to go chase it.

ROGERS HORNSBY
Cardinals infielder

I resent the charges that we intentionally blacked out the city to help save the Yankees. The blackout was an act of God, and even God couldn't save the Yankees.

CONSOLIDATED EDISON SPOKESPERSON

The romance of baseball . . . is in its capacity for stirring fantasy. We are never too old or too bothered to see ourselves wrapping up a World Series victory with a homer in the final inning of the seventh game.

RON FIMRITE
author

Baseball is the only sport I know that when you're on the offense the other team controls the ball.

KEN HARRELSON
Red Sox outfielder

I always wanted to be a player, but I never had the talent to make the big leagues. So I did the next best thing: I bought a team.

CHARLIE FINLEY
Athletics owner

I come, I come, ye have called me long,
I come at the sound of the baseball gong;
I come 'one ball' or 'a strike' to howl,
I come to dodge the bewhiskered foul;
Ye may gaze on my shape as I prance about,
And you bet when I say 'he's out,' he's out.

ANONYMOUS
"Voice of the Umpire"

I put my whole heart and soul into baseball, then, one day, it was all over. When you leave baseball you leave part of your childhood behind.

SANDY VANCE,
Dodgers pitcher
(on his arm going dead)

Catch them off guard. Get them looking for something, then hit them with something else. That's what baseball really is. The element of surprise.

BILLY MARTIN
baseball executive

I felt like my bubble-gum card collection had come to life.

JAMES GARNER

actor
(on speaking at a sports celebrity dinner)

The only real happiness a ballplayer has is when he is playing a ball game and accomplishes something he didn't think he could do.

RING LARDNER
author

Not true at all. Vaseline is manufactured right here in the United States.

DON SUTTON
Dodgers pitcher
(on rumors that he had used a "foreign substance" on the ball)

I see great things in baseball. It's our game—the American game. It will take our people out-of-doors, fill them with oxygen, give them a larger physical stoicism. Tend to relieve us from being a nervous, dyspeptic set. Repair these losses, and be a blessing to us.

WALT WHITMAN
poet

The way to catch a knuckleball is to wait until it stops rolling and then to pick it up.

BOB UECKER
Phillies catcher

One thing I do well is hit fly balls.
There's nothing quite like being able
to hit towering flies. It's not like
writing Beethoven's Ninth, but it's
definitely in the top two.

CHARLES SCHULZ
cartoonist

It's pitching, hitting, and defense that wins. Any two can win. All three make you unbeatable.

JOE GARAGIOLA
major league catcher

What has happened is that all your life you operated businesses in such a way that you could one day afford to buy a baseball team. And then you buy the team and forget all the business practices that enabled you to buy it.

GEORGE STEINBRENNER
Yankees owner

Families go to ballparks and that is why baseball is still our national game.

BILL SHEA
Mets executive

I have a theory: The larger the ball, the less the writing about the sport. There are superb books about golf, very good books about baseball, not many good books about football, and very few good books about basketball. There are no books about beachballs.

GEORGE PLIMPTON
author

The only way to
prove you're a good
sport is to lose.

ERNIE BANKS
Cubs shortstop

Basketball, hockey, and track meets are action heaped upon action, climax upon climax, until the onlooker's responses become deadened. Baseball is for the leisurely afternoons of summer and for the unchanging dreams.

ROGER KAHN
author

You can't steal
second base and
keep one foot on
first.

ANONYMOUS

I don't want to get to know the other guys too well. I might like them, and then I might not want to throw at them.

SAL MAGLIE
Giants pitcher

This is really more fun than being president. I really do love baseball and I wish we could do this out on the lawn every day. I wouldn't even complain if a stray ball came through the Oval Office window now and then.

RONALD REAGAN
fortieth president
of the United States

Above anything else, I hate to lose.

JACKIE ROBINSON
Dodgers infielder

Baseball is the only game you can see on the radio.

PHIL HERSH
sportswriter

If there are bleachers in heaven and a warm sun, that's where you'll find Bill Veeck.

CHARLES KURALT
journalist
(on owner of Chicago White Sox)

It's not whether you win or lose, it's how you play the game.

GRANTLAND RICE
sportswriter

He has a weakness for doubles.

BOBO NEWSOM
Senators pitcher
(on Joe DiMaggio's
hitting)

Baseball is a game of inches.

BRANCH RICKEY
baseball executive

When former president Nixon told Steve Sax he was glad that Sax was over his throwing problems, Sax later recalled, "What was I supposed to say? Glad you got over Watergate?"

S T E V E   S A X
Dodgers second baseman

It's a mere moment
in a man's life
between the all-star
game and an old-
timer's game.

VIN SCULLY
Dodgers broadcaster

They give you a round bat and they throw you a round ball. And they tell you to hit it square.

WILLIE STARGELL
Pirates first baseman

236

It gets late early out there.

YOGI BERRA
Yankees catcher
(on sun glare at Yankee Stadium)

I'd walk through hell in a gasoline suit to keep playing baseball.

PETE ROSE
Reds infielder

There are close to 11 million unemployed and half of them are New York Yankee managers.

JOHNNY CARSON
comedian

He can speak 12 languages but can't hit in any of them.

CRITICISM OF MOE BERG
major league catcher, scholar, and American spy

A couple of years ago they told me I was too young to be President and you were too old to be playing baseball. But we fooled them.

JOHN F. KENNEDY
*thirty-fifth president of the United States
(to forty-two-year-old Stan Musial)*

The hardest thing is not *making* the big leagues. Rather, it is *staying* in the big leagues.

PETE ROSE
Reds infielder

I like my players to be married and in debt. That's the way to motivate them.

ERNIE BANKS
Cubs shortstop

Baseball was one hundred percent of my life.

TY COBB
Tigers outfielder

What difference does the uniform make? You don't hit with it.

YOGI BERRA
baseball manager
(on becoming coach of the Astros)

The best qualification a coach can have is being the manager's drinking buddy.

JIM BOUTON
Yankees pitcher

All I remember about my wedding day in 1967 is that the Cubs lost a double-header.

GEORGE F. WILL
author

When you're in a slump, it's almost as if you look out at the field and it's one big glove.

VANCE LAW
major league infielder

A slump starts in your head and winds up in your stomach. You know that eventually it will happen, and you begin to worry about it. Then you know you're in one. And it makes you sick.

BILLY WILLIAMS
Cubs outfielder

I'm throwing twice as hard as I ever did. It's just not getting there as fast.

LEFTY GOMEZ
Yankees pitcher

If I had to name the number one asset you could have for any sport, I'd say speed. In baseball, all a guy with speed has to do is make contact.

RON FAIRLY
Dodgers infielder

I swing big, with everything I've got. I hit big or I miss big. I like to live as big as I can.

BABE RUTH
Yankees outfielder

Been in this game a hundred years, but I see new ways to lose 'em I never knew existed before.

CASEY STENGEL
Mets manager

The game is supposed to be fun. If you have a bad day, don't worry about it. You can't expect to get a hit every game.

YOGI BERRA
Yankees catcher

I used to send a taxicab to the Almanac Hotel the day he was gonna pitch. I didn't want him to get lost on the way to the stadium.

BABE RUTH
Yankees outfielder
(on George Earnshaw)

Baseball is too much a business to them now. I loved baseball. I ate and slept it. But now the players, instead of picking up the sports page, pick up the *Wall Street Journal*. It's different.

SATCHEL PAIGE
Negro league pitcher

All coaches religiously carry fungo bats in the spring to ward off suggestions that they are not working.

JIM BROSNAN
Reds pitcher

When we lose I can't sleep at night. When we win I can't sleep at night. But when you win you wake up feeling better.

JOE TORRE
Mets manager

It's tomorrow that counts. So you worry all the time. It never ends. Lord, baseball is a worrying thing.

STAN COVELESKI
Indians pitcher

Good pitching will always stop good hitting and vice-versa.

CASEY STENGEL
Mets manager

All ballplayers should quit when it starts to feel as if all the baselines run uphill.

BABE RUTH
Yankees outfielder

I don't want to embarrass any other catcher by comparing him with Johnny Bench.

SPARKY ANDERSON
Reds manager
(on Johnny Bench,
Reds catcher)

It is a game to be savored rather than taken in gulps.

BILL VEECK
baseball executive

I knew it would ruin my arm. But one year of 25-7 is worth five of 15-15.

STEVE STONE
Orioles pitcher
(on his Cy Young season)

Ideally, the umpire should combine the integrity of a Supreme Court justice, the physical agility of an acrobat, the endurance of Job, and the imperturbability of Buddha.

ANONYMOUS

Baseball is like a poker game. Nobody wants to quit when he's losing; nobody wants you to quit when you're ahead.

JACKIE ROBINSON
Dodgers infielder

You can't win them all.

CONNIE MACK
Athletics manager

Baseball is a lot like the army— there aren't many individuals. About the only difference is that baseball players get to stay in nice hotels instead of barracks.

BILL LEE
Red Sox pitcher

Pro sports are a tough business—whether you're in baseball, football, or something else. But when you're running around the bases after hitting a home run or jumping up and down after a touchdown, a little boy comes to the surface.

ROY CAMPANELLA
Dodgers catcher

I'm glad I don't play anymore. I could never learn all those handshakes.

PHIL RIZZUTO
Yankees broadcaster
(former Yankees shortstop)

In football the object is to march into enemy territory and cross his goal. In baseball the object is to go home.

GEORGE CARLIN
comedian

I took the two most expensive aspirins in history.

WALLY PIPP
Yankees first baseman
(on sitting out a game with a headache,
allowing Lou Gehrig into the
Yankees lineup)

I was standing in right field. At first I thought it was another of my migraines, but it was just an earthquake.

JOSÉ CANSECO
A's outfielder
(on the 1989 World Series earthquake)

Isn't it amazing that we're worth
so much on the trading block and
worth so little when we talk salary
with the general manager?

JIM KERN
Rangers pitcher

This game is beautiful. I don't think there's anything in the world that can produce so many emotional highs and lows day in and day out.

BILL FREEHAN
Tigers catcher

Poets are like base-ball pitchers. Both have their moments. The intervals are the tough things.

ROBERT FROST
poet

Catching is much like managing. Managers don't really win games, but they can lose plenty of them. The same way with catching. If you're doing a quality job, you should be almost anonymous.

BOB BOONE
Royals catcher

The good Lord was kind to me. He gave me a strong body, a good right arm, and a weak mind.

DIZZY DEAN
Cardinals pitcher

This is the last pure place where Americans dream. This is the last great arena, the last green arena, where everybody can learn the lessons of life.

MARCUS GIAMATTI
(quoting his father Bart Giamatti, baseball executive)

A good base stealer should make the whole infield jumpy. Whether you steal or not, you're changing the rhythm of the game. If the pitcher is concerned about you, he isn't concentrating enough on the batter.

JOE MORGAN
Reds second baseman

Baseball is something more than a game to an American boy; it is his training field for life work. Destroy his faith in its squareness and honesty and you have destroyed something more; you have planted suspicion of all things in his heart.

JUDGE KENESAW MOUNTAIN LANDIS
baseball commissioner

I've heard of guys going 0 for 15, or 0 for 25, but I was 0 for July.

BOB ASPROMONTE
Astros third baseman

A team is where a boy can prove his courage on his own. A gang is where a coward goes to hide.

MICKEY MANTLE
Yankees outfielder

It also makes it easy for the generations to talk to one another.

JOEL OPPENHEIMER
author
(on baseball)

Cobb lived off the field as though he wished to live forever. He lived on the field as though it was his last day.

BRANCH RICKEY
baseball executive
(on Ty Cobb)

The game of baseball has always been linked in my mind with the mystic texture of childhood, with the sounds and smells of summer nights and with the memories of my father.

DORIS KEARNS GOODWIN
author

Now you get the manager outraging traditionalists like myself when he signs a pitcher and says, "I hope you can give me five good innings." If you pitched only five good innings in the old days you were a bum.

S H I R L E Y   P O V I C H
sportswriter

By and large it is the sport that a foreigner is least likely to take to. You have to grow up playing it, you have to accept the lore of the bubble gum card, and believe that if the answer to the Mays-Snider-Mantle question is found, then the universe will be a simpler and more ordered place.

D A V I D   H A L B E R S T A M
author

I wish I had 10 pitchers with Bo Belinsky's stuff and none with his head.

GENE MAUCH
major league manager

Baseball is continuous, like nothing else among American things, an endless game of repeated summers, joining the long generations of all the fathers and all the sons.

DONALD HALL
poet

I've never been afraid to fail. That's something you have to deal with in reality. I think I'm strong enough as a person to accept failing. But I can't accept not trying.

MICHAEL JORDAN
*Bulls basketball great
(on his bid to make the
Chicago White Sox)*

No club that wins a pennant once is an outstanding club. One which bunches two pennants is a good club. But a team which can win three in a row really achieves greatness.

JOHN J. McGRAW
Giants manager

The guy with the biggest stomach will be the first to take off his shirt at a baseball game.

GLENN DICKEY
author

Our earned-run average looks like the national debt.

CHARLIE FOX
Giants manager

Better make it four. I don't think I can eat eight.

YOGI BERRA
Yankees catcher
(when asked if he wanted his pizza cut
into four or eight slices)

There is always some kid who may be seeing me for the first or last time. I owe him my best.

JOE DiMAGGIO
Yankees outfielder

Any umpire who claims he has never missed a play is . . . well, an umpire.

RON LUCIANO
American League umpire

When you're 21, you're a prospect. When you're 30, you're a suspect.

JIM McGLOTHIN
White Sox pitcher

Guessing what the pitcher is going to throw is 80 percent of being a successful hitter. The other 20 percent is just execution.

HANK AARON
Braves outfielder

This winter I'm working out every day, throwing at a wall. I'm 11-0 against the wall.

JIM BOUTON
Yankees pitcher

Going to bed with a woman never hurt a ball player. It's staying up all night looking for them that does you in.

CASEY STENGEL
baseball executive

Obviously the losers in the strike action taken tonight are the sports fans of America.

BOWIE KUHN
baseball commissioner
(on the 1972 players' strike)

There was a vacancy when I left, and the owners decided to continue with it.

A. B. (HAPPY) CHANDLER
baseball commissioner
(on being replaced by Ford Frick)

Throw strikes. Home plate don't move.

SATCHEL PAIGE
Negro league pitcher

The game of baseball is a clean, straight game, and it summons to its presence everybody who enjoys clean, straight athletics. It furnishes amusement to the thousands and thousands. And I like it for two reasons—first because I enjoy it myself and second, because if by the presence of the temporary first magistrate such a healthy amusement can be encouraged, I want to encourage it.

WILLIAM H. TAFT
twenty-seventh president
of the United States

At a ball game, as in a place of worship, no one is alone in the crowd.

JOHN THORN
author

While visiting Alaska, Yogi Berra turned down mousse for dessert saying, ". . . the meat's too tough, and the horns get stuck in my teeth."

YOGI BERRA
Yankees catcher

I found a delivery in my flaw.

DAN "SINKERBALLER" QUISENBERRY

Royals pitcher

Base stealing for me is another sport all by itself. It's a game within a game. I'm the mouse and the cats are trying to trap me.

MAURY WILLS
Dodgers shortstop

Baseball isn't keeping up with science. Satellites are sending accurate signals from outer space to earth, but coaches still have trouble transmitting signals from third base to home.

ELLIS CLARY
Senators third base coach

The pitcher has got only a ball. I've got a bat. So the percentage in weapons is in my favor and I let the fellow with the ball do the fretting.

HANK AARON
Braves outfielder

Baseball must be a great game to survive the fools who run it.

BILL TERRY
Giants first baseman

How hard is hitting? You ever walk into a pitch-black room full of furniture that you've never been in before and try to walk through it without bumping into anything? Well, it's harder than that.

TED KLUSZEWSKI
Reds first baseman

I can never understand why any-body leaves the game early to beat the traffic. The purpose of baseball is to keep you from caring if you beat the traffic.

BILL VAUGHAN
columnist

There was always Joe DiMaggio. If we had him, we could have won. But the Yankees had him, and he murdered everybody, including us.

JOE CRONIN
Red Sox player and manager

It isn't the high price of stars that is expensive, it's the high price of mediocrity.

BILL VEECK
baseball executive

Pitching is just an illusion. You're dealing with a man's eyes. Make him think he's getting one thing and give him another and you've got him.

ALVIN JACKSON
Red Sox pitching coach

It ain't bragging if you can do it.

DIZZY DEAN
Cardinals pitcher

No one can ever see the ball hit the bat because it's physically impossible to focus your eyes that way. However, when I hit the ball especially hard, I could smell the leather start to burn as it struck the wooden bat.

TED WILLIAMS
Red Sox outfielder

He had such a
beautiful swing, he
even looked good
striking out.

MARK KOENIG
*Yankees shortstop
(on Babe Ruth, Yankees outfielder)*

I'm just a ballplayer with one ambition, and that is to give all I've got to help my ball club win. I've never played any other way.

JOE DIMAGGIO
Yankees outfielder

It is an American institution and more lasting than some marriages, war, Supreme Court decisions, and even major depressions.

ART RUST
Indians third baseman

You can't tell how much spirit a team has until it starts losing.

ROCKY COLAVITO
Tigers outfielder

Batting practice is the time to stand around in the outfield and tell each other stories.

JIM BOUTON
Yankees pitcher

You don't save a pitcher for tomorrow. Tomorrow it may rain.

LEO DUROCHER
baseball executive

If Ben Franklin played shortstop here and made an error, they'd probably boo him for a week, too.

RUSS HODGES
broadcaster
(on the Phillies fans)

If they did get a machine to replace us, you know what would happen to it? Why, the players would bust it to pieces every time it ruled against them. They'd clobber it with a bat.

HARRY WENDELSTEDT
National League umpire

The beauty and joy
of baseball is not
having to explain it.

CHUCK SHRIVER
Cubs publicist

Next to religion, baseball has furnished a greater impact on American life than any other institution.

HERBERT HOOVER
*thirty-first president
of the United States*

No little boy in the hospital asked me to hit one, I didn't promise it to my kid for his birthday, and my wife will be too shocked to appreciate it. I hit it for me.

ROCKY BRIDGES
major league utility man
(on hitting his first homer in
two seasons)

Though it is a team game by definition, it is actually a series of loosely connected individual efforts.

BILL VEECK
baseball executive

You argue with the umpire because there's nothing else you can do about it.

LEO DUROCHER
baseball executive

Ruth made a grave mistake when he gave up pitching. Working once a week, he might have lasted a long time and become a great star.

TRIS SPEAKER
Indians player and manager
(on Babe Ruth becoming a
Yankees outfielder)

Sliding headfirst is the safest way to get to the next base, I think. And the fastest. You don't lose your momentum . . . and there's one more important reason I slide headfirst. It gets my picture in the paper.

PETE ROSE
Reds infielder

One day you can throw tomatoes through brick walls. The next day you can't dent a pane of glass with a rock. It hurts but you hang on, hoping it'll come back. Oh, well, it's a helluva ride, the one on the way up.

DEAN CHANCE
Angels pitcher

I'd rather hit home runs. You don't have to run as hard.

DAVE KINGMAN
Mets first baseman

If I knew exactly what I know now and had it to do over, I'd be a switch hitter. No telling what I could have done.

HANK AARON
Braves outfielder

I was never nervous when I had the ball, but when I let it go I was scared to death.

LEFTY GOMEZ
Yankees pitcher

Ninety feet between home plate and first base may be the closest man has ever come to perfection.

RED SMITH
sportswriter

All baseball fans are provincial. They don't want the best team to win. They want *their* team to win.

ART HILL
author

He'd give you the shirt off his back. Of course, he'd call a press conference to announce it.

JIM "CATFISH" HUNTER
Yankees pitcher
(on Reggie Jackson)

A pitcher needs two pitches—one they're looking for and one to cross 'em up.

WARREN SPAHN
Braves pitcher

A baseball manager is a necessary evil.

SPARKY ANDERSON
Reds manager

The space between the white lines—that's my office. That's where I conduct my business.

EARLY WYNN
Indians pitcher

You give 100 percent in the first half of the game, and if that isn't enough in the second half you give what's left.

YOGI BERRA
Yankees catcher

There are only two places in this league. First place and no place.

TOM SEAVER
Mets pitcher

Any minute, any day, some players may break a long-standing record. That's one of the fascinations about the game—the unexpected surprises.

CONNIE MACK
Athletics manager

There isn't enough mustard in the world to cover that hot dog.

DAROLD KNOWLES
A's pitcher
(on Reggie Jackson)

To compare baseball with other team games is to say the Hope Diamond is a nice chunk of carbon. The endless variety of physical and mental skills demanded by baseball is both uncomparable and incomparable.

BILL VEECK
baseball executive

If you don't play to win, why keep score?

VERNON LAW
Pirates pitcher

Hitting the ball was easy. Running around the bases was the tough part.

MICKEY MANTLE
Yankees outfielder

He's so good, I
even worry about
him in the winter.

TED WILLIAMS
Red Sox outfielder
(on Bob Lemon)

When we win, I'm so happy I eat a lot. When we lose, I'm so depressed, I eat a lot. When we're rained out, I'm so disappointed I eat a lot.

TOMMY LASORDA
Dodgers manager

The majority of American males put themselves to sleep by striking out the batting order of the New York Yankees.

JAMES THURBER
author

People don't blink when Paul Newman gets paid millions to make a movie, or Frank Sinatra to sing. Why not a ballplayer? It's like a lot of other professions. The money is just there.

RAY BOONE
Tigers infielder

Talent always beats experience. Because by the time you get experience, the talent's gone.

PAT CORRALES
Indians manager

I didn't come to New York to be a star. I brought my star with me.

REGGIE JACKSON
Yankees outfielder
(upon arriving in New York in 1977)

Most pitchers are too smart to manage.

JIM PALMER
Orioles pitcher

Baseball is the only game in America for normal people. To play basketball, you have to be seven-feet-six. To play football, you have to have the same width.

BILL VEECK
baseball executive

My mother must have sent them my baby picture; that was the last time I weighed 175.

CHARLIE KERFELD
Astros pitcher
(responding to the fact that he was listed on his baseball card as 5'11" and 175 lbs, when he was actually 6'6" and 245 lbs.)

You're only as smart as your ERA.

JIM BOUTON
Yankees pitcher

I have discovered, in twenty years of moving around the ballpark, that the knowledge of the game is usually in inverse proportion to the price of the seats.

BILL VEECK
baseball executive

Our 1976 White Sox team was so bad that by the fifth inning Bill Veeck was selling hot dogs to go.

KEN BRETT
White Sox pitcher

I never questioned the integrity of an umpire. Their eyesight, yes.

LEO DUROCHER
baseball executive

The clock doesn't matter in baseball. Time stands still or moves backward. Theoretically, one game could go on forever. Some seem to.

HERB CAEN
author

When you come right down to it, the baseball owners are really little boys with big wallets.

HAROLD PARROTT
baseball executive

There is but one game, and that game is baseball.

JOHN J. MCGRAW
Giants manager

Baseball can build you up to the sky one day and the next day you have to climb a stepladder to look up to a snake.

JOHNNY PESKY
Red Sox manager

Nothing makes a pitcher feel more secure than the sight of his teammates circling the bases during a ball game.

JIM BROSNAN
Reds pitcher

Whitey and I figured out once that each year I hit about fifteen long outs at Yankee Stadium that would have been home runs at Ebbets Field. In my eighteen years I would have gotten 270 additional home runs if I'd been a Dodger.

MICKEY MANTLE
Yankees outfielder

I became a good pitcher
when I stopped trying to make
them miss the ball and started
trying to make them hit it.

S A N D Y   K O U F A X
Dodgers pitcher

I'd like to thank the good Lord for making me a Yankee.

JOE DIMAGGIO
Yankees outfielder

This team, it all flows from me. I've got to keep it going. I'm the straw that stirs the drink.

REGGIE JACKSON
Yankees outfielder

The text of this book was set in

Palatino and Princetown by Junie Lee.

———————

Book design by

Judith Stagnitto Abbate